M000020903

GRAVEDIGGER'S
BIRTHDAY

8/4/04

For Sandy Ozgar

Teacher

A gardener over
our most important
seeds

—B

ALSO BY BJ WARD

Landing in New Jersey with Soft Hands
17 Love Poems with No Despair

GRAVEDIGGER'S BIRTHDAY

POEMS BY

~~BJ WARD~~

North Atlantic Books
Berkeley, California

Copyright © 2002 by BJ Ward. All rights reserved. No portion of this book, except for brief review, may be reproduced, stored in a retrieval system, or transmitted in any form or by any means — electronic, mechanical, photocopying, recording or otherwise — without the written permission of the publisher. For information contact North Atlantic Books.

Published by
North Atlantic Books
P.O. Box 12327
Berkeley, California 94712

Printed in the United States of America

Cover and book design: © jcampstudio.com

Cover illustration: Brian Rumbolo, www.brianrumbolo.com

Author photo: Michèle Souter, www.dvibe.com/shelly

BJ Ward's website can be found at http://bjward.olsain.com
    It is provided courtesy of Olsain Web Services.

Gravedigger's Birthday is sponsored by the Society for the Study of Native Arts and Sciences, a nonprofit educational corporation whose goals are to develop an educational and crosscultural perspective linking various scientific, social, and artistic fields; to nurture a holistic view of arts, sciences, humanities, and healing; and to publish and distribute literature on the relationship of mind, body, and nature.

North Atlantic Books' publications are available through most bookstores. For further information, call 800-337-2665 or visit our website at www.northatlanticbooks.com.

Substantial discounts on bulk quantities are available to corporations, professional associations, and other organizations. For details and discount information, contact our special sales department.

Library of Congress Cataloging-in-Publication Data

Ward, B. J., 1967–
    Gravedigger's Birthday : poems / by BJ Ward.
        p. cm.
    ISBN 1-55643-422-7 (pbk)
    1. Title.
PS3573.A693 G73 2002
811'.54—dc21   2002009793
                                                        CIP

1 2 3 4 5 6 7 8 9 / 06 05 04 03 02

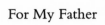

For My Father

Contents

"The longer you live
the sooner you bloody-well die."

> —from "Isn't It Grand," *Traditional Irish Song, as sung by Tommy Makem and the Clancy Brothers*

"Has this fellow no feeling of his business, that he sings at grave-making?"

> —from *Hamlet* (Act V, sc. i), *William Shakespeare*

"We even flew a little."

> —from "A Pity. We Were Such a Good Invention," *Yehuda Amichai (translated by Assia Gutmann)*

287 was the long road to the newspaper plant
    my black-handed father would ride beneath
the weight of a night sky.
    A father who works the night shift
knows that weight, how it accumulates from within
    when his mistakes and debt
begin to press on his children and wife.
    And so went his life —

If the stars spelled something real,
    they might spell the equation
that my father never mastered —
    the news just ran through his hands
and what slid there left the black residue
    of the world's doings, pressed knowledge
that read like misaligned tea leaves in his hardening palms,
    and in his life line and heart line and other lines
that would normally speak a fortune,
    the night just accumulated itself—
a little sky he would spread over us
    when the world redelivered him in the morning.

Gravedigger's Birthday

We had only dated for three weeks
but there I was, burying her cat.
To top things off, it was my birthday,
but I knew the cat's death trumped it
so into the ground I went,
never having dug a grave before
but knowing I should know how.
Such an ancient, simple action,
as if our bodies evolved to do such work —
opposable thumb to dig and dig
deeper into the earth, and standing erect
to toss soil from our graves. I remembered
something from somewhere — boy scouts
or horror movie — delve deep enough
so raccoons can't stir up the corpse.
I did it all quietly with a sudden solemnity
not for the cat — I barely knew it —
but for the motion, the first ancestral thing
I had done in years, aware this was traffic
with old gods. The indifferent stars pinned
the lips of the grave open, and I lifted up
that solid eggplant of a body, and lowered her
carefully into the soil, as if the cat could feel it,
or the earth could. Ridiculous.
Then I lifted up that shovel, again
knowing what to do — load upon load
into the earth, back onto that body,
returning it but also casting it out
of my modern life where I would soon take

the short walk from the grave to the house,
eat some meat without thinking
of eating the meat, get in bed
next to my new, warm, mourning girlfriend
on a mattress imported from far away, some speck
of the grave's dirt rising behind a fingernail
as I lie awake, the faint next click
of my life's odometer there in the darkness,
living and dying at the same time,
thinking how so much motion and instinct
lies inert in the earth next to the swing set,
and how the ground's new toothless mouth
settled into closure without pomp,
temporary and permanent at once.

Education

When Mary and I finally decided we were old
    enough to make love, we needed to find a spot
to park the Datsun.
    Two high school students, we were full
of what the world had not yet offered us.
    Achievement's taste constantly dissolved
under our barely used tongues.
    We approached our old grammar school —
its parking lot spread out
    like an asphalt puddle that had leaked
from the foundation of our early education,
    hardening into something we could anchor on.
We coupled there, the school rising
    above the shifting car. We were lost
in the universe contained in a Datsun —
    everything we had ever learned
was an opaque wall we hid behind
    as we embraced the greatest lesson
there were no instructions for,
    only blanks to fill in
as we discovered them, no wrong answers
    in the multiple choices,
feeling both lost and found at once — we
    were each Columbus, each the other's New World.
Our transmission hovered
    over a hopscotch outline,
the slight chalk markings
    that had once told us where to go,
where not to. It would be years
    before I knew what I learned.

Emperor

I was eighteen. The Garden State Parkway.
The police car in the bushes of the meridian,
its red light bar like an eyelid suddenly
opening, six eyes flashing about wildly,
looking for me.

"It's an ambush," I thought.
Me, who had my whole empire
in control — even the hairs on my head
were soldiers standing in order, helping me conquer
what I thought I had to own.

I was eighteen. The gas pedal was like all
physical things, destined to fall downward.
And now I confess
I don't remember anything
about the ticket — its cost or the cop

whose hand wrote my birth name
in the tiny squares, incorporating
my identity into the system.
In years I'd know he was just
doing what he had to do — as was I.

"Here's your ticket," he said,
as if he were an usher
whose job was to rip things in half.
"What am I entering?" I thought.
So my empire began to fall on a shoulder

of the Garden State Parkway —
not usurped, really, but undermined.
I was eighteen and falling
through society's turnstiles —
college, speed limits, combing my hair

into a daily unnoticeable —
a work of art whose strength
was that it didn't particularly stand out,
like driving well. I drove off,
pushing the accelerator pedal

to the exact angle of, say,
the Tower of Pisa.
How I wanted to topple it.
How it became the only thing in my world
that could ever rise back.

Spring Begins in Hinckley, Ohio

For the past 41 years, the town of Hinckley, Ohio, has waited patiently for what it considers the first true indication that spring is here—the return of the buzzards. For four decades now, a flock of buzzards—also known as turkey vultures—returns each March 15 to Hinckley's rocky ledges. And this year, despite a blowing snow and sub-freezing temperatures, the buzzards did not disappoint.

—CNN (March 15, 1998)

I

I am sure the axis of the earth
passes through Hinckley, Ohio,
because every year the buzzards drop down—
little flags of death
lowered on an ancient flagpole—
and people rejoice.
The town runs out of champagne.
How appropriate to cherish
the reinstated balance of the world—
vultures corkscrewing down as tulips squeeze
themselves open—a wrenching into tenderness—
and spring herself starts teasing out the grasses,
tuning up the wind's motor, airing out the willows' drapes,
setting up summer's bright, unlocked house.
And with life rising and eternity dropping,
Hinckley's people become suddenly and quite happily caught again
between a contralto and baritone singing the same song.

II

I am east of Hinckley—northwestern New Jersey,
where for some reason the world is still still
and warmth is a love letter on the way
via bulk rate. However, the teethed cold

outside the car can't keep this sky from blushing
as I ride partially into it, partially out of it.
Here everything outdoors is locked frozen,
but what compels me are the worms
deep beneath the ice — those puny and insistent ground vultures,
little squirming letters that spell a frightening word —
the worms who have been eating decayed
hands, buried waste, swallowing dog turds
as if they were éclairs. To have that hunger for waste —
to blindly eat the rusting rainbow taffeta
of last year's leaves. . . . I love how they love
what is used and then spoiled — how they, deep
in their wormy brains, must know that death is a factory
always in production, always in the black,
and how they set up their pantry there,
beneath the cold, immersed in the earth
where we'll all return when we are done
driving, done waitressing or practicing law,
done with grieving and done with loving
what is passing, done with eating whatever
death we eat and justify with our own vulture logic.

III

People of Hinckley celebrate one thing in two halves:
while the world opens its wide garage doors again
to thoughts of rebirth, bumper crops, and long summer kisses,
above and below us there is an ancestral motion
scribbling its uneasy language
against the sky and in the earth,

                  its ancient hand slowly spelling, as if in no rush,
Bring it all back through my body.

8

Daily Grind

A man awakes every morning
and instead of reading the newspaper
reads Act V of Othello.
He sips his coffee and is content
that this is the news he needs
as his wife looks on helplessly.
The first week she thought it a phase,
his reading this and glaring at her throughout,
the first month an obsession,
the first year a quirkiness in his character,
and now it's just normal behavior,
this mood setting in over the sliced bananas,
so she tries to make herself beautiful
to appease his drastic taste.
And every morning, as he shaves
the stubble from his face, he questions everything—
his employees, his best friend's loyalty,
the women in his wife's canasta club,
and most especially the wife herself
as she puts on lipstick in the mirror next to him
just before he leaves. This is how he begins
each day of his life—as he tightens the tie
around his neck, he remembers the ending,
goes over it word by word in his head,
the complex drama of his every morning
always unfolded on the kitchen table,
a secret Iago come to light with every sunrise
breaking through his window, the syllables
of betrayal and suicide always echoing
as he waits for his car pool, just under his lips
even as he pecks his wife goodbye.

Roy Orbison's Last Three Notes

12 mph over the speed limit on Route 80, I realize
the way I know the exact size of my bones
is the way I know I am the only one
in America listening to Roy Orbison
singing "Blue Bayou" at this precise moment,
and I feel sorry for everyone else.
Do they realize they are missing
his third from last note?—*Bluuuueee*—
and how it becomes a giant mouth I'm driving into—
"Bay"—pronounced *bi*—becomes the finger
pointing back—*biiiiiiii*—and all the sealed up cars
greasing along this dirty, pot-holed clavicle of New Jersey
don't know this "you"—constant as my exhaust smoke—
yooooouuuu—and the beats underneath, more insistent
than the landlord knocking on the door—horns, drums, guitar, bass—
my Toyota Corolla is now one serious vehicle,
and the band and I are all alone now, filling it up—
Roy and me in our cool sunglasses up front
and his musicians barely fitting their instruments in the back,
driving into the blue—bom bom bom—pulling ahead
of the pollution faster than New Jersey can spit it out—
Bye—boom bom—his leggy background singers must be jammed
in the trunk because suddenly I hear them and suddenly
we are Odysseus and his boys bringing the Sirens with us,
and the cassette player is our black box
containing all essential details in case we don't make it,
but I know we're going to make it
because Roy Orbison turns to me
and says, like the President says to his top general

after a war has been won, or like Morgan Earp
on his deathbed said to Wyatt when vengeance
was up to him, or like Gretchen Honecker
said when I knew I was about to get my first kiss,
Roy turns to me and says, *"You—"*

Christmas Eve, 1975: What I Realize Now

I: *My Mother, the Waitress: The 3 to 11 Shift*

The repairmen winked at her,
    an executive pinched her ass.
This is how her tips grew large

all evening long, just as the savings
    had grown large for our gifts —
the savings that Father blew on gin & Bud

a little every day in November
    until only zeroes were left
for her eyes. She was working to buy

a watch for me, a horn for Tiny, Rockem-Sockem
    for both of us. If she could pull
30 more dollars she could get these three gifts

and the K-Mart was open til midnight.
    She was doing all sorts of shifts
to make everyone happy.

It was love, Christmas, and love
    was something we learned from Mother.
We learned Christmas from Mom.

II: *My Father: Out of Beer, It Must Be Our Fault*

It was love, Christmas, and love
    rained down from stars
as Father's hands rained on us.

His fist was cold and constructed
    over years of labor — his breath was death
and, this being Christmas Eve, death was what he celebrated

in his own fatherly ways. He smashed
    himself into liquor and then smashed
that liquor into us. I ran

through the den, the din
    following, almost engulfing me.
Tiny hid beneath the tree,

the lights blinking a wild electricity,
    circuits clicking, my father reaching
beneath the ornaments, unwrapping

his belt. There beneath the mistletoe
    the buckle kissed my brother's cheek
and I yelled to hell with Christmas

and shoved the tree over. Father chased,
     stumbled, and my brother and I burst
through the door like wounded deer,

darting into the cold snow and unknown
     presents the dark offered. But no —
it wasn't dark. We had each other,

and we ran through starlight.

III: *My Brother and I: Clearing the Stream*

The drainage pipe was clogged with autumn-
     worn debris & leaves and held
our stream with this ugly, thick tongue.

We started tugging, pulling handfuls of dead
     wood from our water, which we needed to clear.
Our father was drunk, violent, and yelling

for us. His voice echoed in the dark woods.
     Hand over hand we yanked a hole
through the accumulations of a hard fall,

each encouraging the other, saying,
     We can't get hurt. It's Christmas Eve,
while our hands froze with each plunge

into garbage. Once the water was freed,
    we could hide in the safe, cold pipe,
whose only echoes would be ours.

When Mother arrived home, her pockets emptied
    but hands full of the three gifts
she stumbled over something in the living room.

Father was passed out, using the fallen tree
    as a pillow, belt still in hand. She waited
all night for us, afraid to call the police,

not knowing we were shivering in the pipe,
    the echoes still looming about us,
blow-down zones in our eyes, and hugging,

giving each other Christmas,
    thinking, if we could wait it out,
how great Christmas morning would be —

there would be the delightful sound of bells,
    an angel's voice, maybe.
Maybe just a little quiet after.

Bastards with Badges

A bottle was never more tyrannous
than when smashed against the wall
behind my mother. She left Him,

taking us with her, and for five nights
we slept in the rotting frame of her Chevy Impala,
shipwrecked on the dark shore of the Acme parking lot.

Now Bradford says to me,
"All cops are bastards with badges"—
some acid laced with vanilla truth.

I know how power could be a siren song
that outseduces the sense of justice, just an ocean
cops float on with its monotonous sounds.

And I know there are no words to describe for Bradford
the precise smell of the Impala's rug
as I lay over the transmission hump

behind the long front seat, my brother tossing
on the vinyl specimen board of the back seat, tossing
in the tidal wave of fear that moved all night through the Chevrolet.

How can I explain to Bradford that there was a cop car
poised at the far end of the lot like a storm waiting to approach—
kept at bay by some invisible high pressure system?

I hated those cops, those salivating hybrids
of sharks and dobermans who faced us all night,
making sure we didn't steal. Everyone knew my family.

How can I explain that they *were* watching us,
some kind of angels with guns, cherry-topped lighthouses
as we drifted across dark, unknown currents —

guardians of the asphalt — for once, we had guardians —
all of us prone in the car, stretched between
locked doors, so far from the darkening sky

that was always in our house, so close
to the driveshaft, for five safe nights —
and I looked at my beautiful mother,

a first mate suddenly forced to be captain
of a ship out of control and already half-wrecked,
my beautiful mother, her sleeping head right

between the steering wheel and gas pedal,
as if her dreams could drive us towards dawn.
The sun eventually smashed through our windows,

glimmering like the sky's shiny new badge.
I surveyed our survival — the cops were gone,
just the three of us lying flat out on our possessions.

Above us all rose my mother's hand, dangling from the column shifter
like some battle-tattered flag for independence, surrounded
by the glass shards and quietude of a parking lot gone empty.

My beautiful mother, safer than ever before,
even in defection. ¼ tank of gas, fully empowered,
her car pointed in every direction.

Upon Being Told Again There Are No Rhymes
For Certain Words

Crossing to my studio eighty yards
through some briars, I lug a verbal freight:
both volumes of the New Shorter Oxford
English Dictionary. I contemplate
a carpenter bringing a lumber pile
to his wood shop—I want to build structures
from words that readers could live in awhile.
I know it's rare, tricky stuff, such scripture—
umpteen poets, still no rhymes for purple.
Bonds could beat McGuire and Ruth—but orange?
I'd reconstruct Heaven, or usurp Hell—
write till I swing open like a door hinge.
I arrive—a rogue who'd refurbish town.
I take my pen, begin to nail things down.

The Noises I Make

(for Doug Boyce)

My friend hears me in the shower singing
Tom Waits' "The Piano Has Been Drinking"

at 8:15 a.m. A composer,
he critiques me. "Maybe the tongue throes, or

the timing, or the pitch, the inflections."
I don't care—I rejoice in my imperfections.

I lift my shirt and scratch my belly
for the cause of impropriety.

I snore at night; my lungs are just big toys—
even when I sleep, I make all the wrong noise.

New Jersey

Whenever friends visit from far away —
San Francisco or Jamaica —
what amazes them about my state
more than the long couch of the shore
looking at the constant television of the ocean
or the cloverleaf exit ramps swirling out
like ribbons about to be tightened
on the gift of traffic congestion —
what amazes them are the groundhogs —
"What a noble creature," George said.
"Holy crow, mon, a land seal," said Billson.
And there it is — a stubby, little, near-sighted Buddha
looking up from the county road's bank
as we stop the car, reverse back to it.
If we were all in a bar in Bayonne,
its look would say, "I'm gonna kick your ass."
In a library, it would say, "Why are you
disturbing me? I'm reading Kirkegaard."
But this is the weedy hips of the thoroughfare,
and our friend is mid-sentence in the grass's long summer novel,
navigating its own cloverleaves. It considers us
in our ridiculous car, and then something amazing —
it stands up on its hind legs — and I realize
the Jersey water has helped it evolve
into something more human.
This is New Jersey.
We're crawling on four wheels backwards,
looking at its pinched face,
the shimmering flanks, the dehydrated hands —
the short, imperfect loveliness of groundhog.

After I Read Sandy Zulauf's "Across the Bar," Victoria Takes Me Skiing

I don't even like how it looks, Sandy —
the word "skiing" —
with that double i, like twin daggers
jutting from the word's deep pockets
towards me.
Vowels are supposed to be flowing and feminine —
consonants, guttural and male.
But these i's have their own grammar.
There they are —
Victoria would say they look like skis,
your wife Madeline might say ski poles,
but I say they are twin stilettos
that have already killed a consonant
that used to be there.

And I like even less the act itself.
Sandy, guys like us should trudge,
barrel, invade, whack away weeds with machetes —
but Madeline and Victoria tried to get us
to flow, to work easily across this new skin from the sky.
I know what their circular, beautiful
woman logic is saying to them:
that we're poets, we're used
to spreading easily across white surfaces,
making our way from one margin to the other
and leaving marks —
that our tracks are like cursive writings across a field,
the pokings of ski poles
like punctuation that helps us pace.

In short, they tried to kill us, Sandy.
So I offer them this poem,
written in curses and cursive,
and here I think I actually got somewhere,
like the beer that slalomed down my throat
as I watched Victoria finish her skiing,
a skating clef along the musical note tree line,
looking absolutely lovely against the fresh snow
like the perfect word in a poem as you write it—
the trails behind her like the echoes of that word
that remain after you've moved on,

                                    a double pleasure,
or perhaps the trails are a double i
flowing behind her pretty legs,
us men just consonants on the outside.

Reloading the Stapler

Little bucktoothed alligator
ready to taste my bills.

Make something suffer.
Make something stick.

Bandages

—One week after my student is raped.

In the hallway while classes were in session
my student quietly confided to me,
shaking like a lake in an earthquake.
She began to break down and in three seconds
moved her hands quickly enough to shield
her face, then chest, then opposite forearms,
as if trying to cover a huge country with body parts,
or the shadows of them. Then she burst
her arms open and threw herself upon me,
murmuring she had only told her two best friends
before me and then her head was buried
in my chest and I put my arms around her
tentatively, looking over her shoulders
to see if anyone could see us. I wanted to shove her
away, thinking of my job, of headlines,
of how this kind of comfort was outside
the behavioral guidelines of my contract.
She began to sob more softly while holding me
tightly, and I let her. I let her have control
of me for that moment. I let her break
behavioral guidelines as more important ones
had been broken on her. And then we stopped
being student and teacher—just people
at a loss when the powerful and unexpected
had been suddenly thrust upon us.
The principal and three students turned the corner
and stopped short. I knew it might be years
before I cleared my name, but far longer

for her to reclaim her life. *"Mr. Ward!"*
from the principal's thick throat, crashing
down the hall, drawing teachers out
just like echoes from their doorways. *Mr. Ward!*
Mr. Ward! I had already closed my eyes
and could smell her hair. Sweet. She had stopped
sobbing and we hugged in silence.
As they drew closer, she tightened
so I did too. We were as quiet and taut as bandages
upon each other. Yes, I squeezed her tighter
as the whole world pressed in on us.

The Suicidologist

He sees in everyone's bodies
the possibility to cast shadows—
finds it so hard
to enjoy himself
at a cocktail party,
all the ladies in their pretty dresses
just covering up some tumult,
some neediness just short of collapsing
into itself.
In the park, on a sunny day at noon,
he looks at all the happy people
standing over the dark spot of themselves
that will surely lengthen
to be bigger than their own bodies
as the day wears itself against them.
As children we learned our shadow
is a darkness we never totally shake
until we lie down, pull the shades,
draw the curtains, shut out the world,
and turn our own light out.

Sunrise, Sunset

Such a bright dark
tune, the chorus reprising
like the celestial cycle itself,
but the song doesn't quite account
for how unstoppably the sunrise barrels ·
toward us out of the starting gate of the East,
billowing, roiling—an eternally budding fireflower—
and how, after it has incessantly hissed its arias of light
and suffused our gardens with its cargo, soaring overhead
like our earth's nuclear-powered, juggernautish crop-duster
as the austere clouds slide steadfastly across the sky like drunks
trying to maintain their dignity while they escape the last-call flood-
light the bartender has ineluctably switched on, O how the sun
every evening finally settles on the tops of the farthest
western mountains and becomes a fiddler
on a distant neighbor's roof, virtuosic
in the day's final encore, his strings on fire,
and jumps off into the ocean
to put them out.

The 18th Poem

(after Tom Waits)

Small print on a contract
was the ugliest thing you invented.
"I love you" was our pact
in big letters, as if you intended

to honor those words, inhabit that city.
I love you— what else was there to say?
And then your whisper of infidelity —
o how the small print taketh away —

The Poems I Regret In My First Book

Irretractable, obnoxious children
    having tantrums on the dog-eared tabletops
of these pages, screaming out,
    "Failure! Failure!"
in an otherwise classy joint.
    Words I wrote so long ago
while drunk perhaps, or worse, young —
    subversive little syllables that slipped
my editor's eyes, smuggled in, cloaked
    by the good, rightly-legal stuff —
now conspiring to kill the whole book
    with ugliness.
There they are — irrevocable
    in their deficiencies, the runts of the litter
making the most noise,
    whom I can't punish by banishing
to the room of "Out of Print"
    without sequestering the good children as well.
(This is how books called *Selected Poems* are born.)

So here I am, in front of an audience,
    peddling a volume that should be half-quarantined,
not reading certain pieces,
    keeping those kids on the bench
while about nine players swing for the fence
    and hopefully carry the team.

For Those Who Grew Up on a River

(for Frank Niccoletti)

Brethren of muck and trout —
sultans of pike and pollywog —
clasping ropes that swung over wispy reflections
we'd shatter with our summer bodies.
We look at the world
as one long page
with fluid sentences
running across it.
I remember how the river bebopped
to its own insistent aria,
a motion whose seduction
was challenged only

by Janey's lucid summer dress
which waved to me unbearably.
I left rafts and inner tubes
for Chevies, Plymouths, anything
with a motor to take me
down asphalt estuaries,
Janey at my side,
accelerating toward an ocean
of credit and responsibility.
I felt then
the river was what I'd leave behind,
drift into the world of skyscrapers
and my children's dance lessons.
How hard it was to learn
motors fail. Romance dies.

My river compatriots,
maybe only you understand this:

the more rocks we hit,
the louder we sing.
Janey's long gone.
The river still kisses me.

Filling in the New Address Book

But rifling through the old one,
choosing whom to preserve
in your encyclopedia of associates,
whom to let become obsolete —
no room for them in your entire world.
You little god, you,
you puny pocket of omnipotence —
how you throw people off the side
of your dinghy-book,
a tiny captain thinking, "This is dead weight."
Old girlfriends — doubly gone now.
Old drinking buddies, married and laden
with responsibility, that grand soberer.
So you continue, you infinitesimal infinite one,
scratching out the names of the dead,
people you are coming from and never toward,
tearing down street signs, phone lines,
upheaving entire highways between you
as you leave them out,
their new and unfamiliar lives
not any less full than if you included them.
They are manning their own ships and,
sorry little god,
no room for you on their voyage either.
It's understood, no? You've been heroes together
in the past lives within this life —
Ulysseses now full of uselessnesses —
and why threaten any miraculous history,
any great testament, with knowledge
of how empty your current book of stories is?

My Mother's Last Cigarette

(for His Holiness, Pope John Paul II—March 2000)

So now You have apologized to everyone in the world
except my mother. Your mouth opened like cathedral doors
beneath the pure untouched steeple of your hat
and *I'm sorry*'s flung out like shiny coins being tossed
into the baskets of people's ears. Except my mother's.

Keep all those apologies — shine them up
and pray to them if you will.
I want 1979. Rescind 1979. Give me back 1979
and your wide absence from my mother's needs,
your wide endorsement of her ignoble sorrow.
Give me back the seeds of ghosts sown in her eyes
when the priests told her to take it —
to take the absence of her own-taken husband,
to somehow— wrong as it was and a pity tsk a pity —
to take the fists that were mountains bad gods lived on —
take their arcs which traced a demon's wing on his right,
an angel's back on his left — take the bear hugs
and take them again, to take and to hold they said,
to pray for him and all the husbands who have gone astray.

I said give me back my mother's eyes
when your priests, all of them, told her she was married
before God and God was watching
and she must pray harder. And we did.
We did.
We prayed and made our hands campfires

hot with wishes pointed toward heaven,
pushed our palms together like pressing machines
that might press those wishes into prayers
beautiful enough for angels to pick up
and carry to our Lord—

I said rescind 1979,
when the entire world outside our house
was popping pills, creating little disco floors
with little lights flashing in everyone's suddenly pink brains,
everyone except my mother, sober as a burnt-down church,
kneeling at the kitchen table,
cracked tooth, hands letting go
of the repo notice, too afraid to see the doctor,
your priests her only last option. I said rescind it.
Rescind it all— the haematomas, the priests' cocksure
refutations that now stood between my weeping mother and
Jesus's wide embrace. Rescind it now. Rescind 1979
and I'll forget how she looked ornate in her misery and bruises
and how she picked up her Newports
and lit her last cigarette, nowhere to turn—
your churches nothing but walls
our personal tyrant could hide behind—

but you can't.
You can't rescind her last cigarette
and black eyes and empty pockets and good Catholic shame
for not being a better wife— the priests said to be a better wife—
nor can you rescind her two sons learning to cry without noise,

looking at her through a hole punched in the wall.
And you have no power to rescind the 3 white puffs of smoke
they saw rising from her, coronating a new secular holiness
in our vast and troubled land.

Burying Father

In Seaside Heights, NJ, my father would shade us
with his huge beer belly that curved down
over the copper snap of his red cut-offs.
My brother and I found refuge from the sun there,
beneath the frame that was a delight to bury.
He stood over us for the length of digging,
positioning so his shadow would shelter us.
The surface sand was easiest, ran through our hands
quicker than dimes as the ocean registered
the latest items of its ancient complaint. Then
the lower soil, compact, years of compression
(what did we know of compression?), harder
to get through, pull up, finally discard. We knew our father
wouldn't fit in any shallow ditch — too immense
for that easy burial — and so in the darkness we pushed.
Back then I hadn't read much but I had read about treasures
in *Boy's Life,* all sorts of value too deep for detectors,
covered by years of tidal shifts and wind's constant backhoe.
We never found anything. How I miss those days now —
in 25 years, my brother and I would be friends
who hardly speak, but in those days we'd shovel together,
doing our best to bury Dad. How we enjoyed his shadow —
a good darkness then — never thinking about the unhealthiness
of such an imposing frame, or anything as grave.

Another Poem on the Death of a Dog

The Greeks had the Oracle at Delphi —
a holy place where supplications were granted;
you had the refrigerator.
The sound of the cold cut drawer sliding open
equal in your world
to the Berlin Wall coming down in mine,
and you started your little funk dance,
as in your head, in some dog language,
the words were formed: *which meat?*
which meat? which meat?(or is it cheese?)
and your tail became your body's metronome —
a tail so beguiling I've seen you chase it
as if it were the chalice of Christ
and you a manic crusading knight.
So poor, you didn't even
have pockets.
And your stubby, flea-bitten
legs — how they kicked
when you slept.
Were you dreaming
that they were longer?
Or perhaps you were dancing
with a poodle somewhere in a dog bar
where they served dog drinks
and you could dip your snout
into the finger bowl of biscuits
the dogtender put out
to make all the customers thirstier?
In truth, you were a good dog, old friend,

purer in intention than any man.
What about all the murder? people might ask.
I tell them your tongue was democratic,
eager to accept all — from moth to woodchuck.
I tell the cosmos' jury that I saw you
let the cat go. That on this earth
you even shared the water bowl
with your greatest enemy.
I tell them how each whisker on your face
grew into a little divining rod.
I tell them all how your body was a duct
with pure instinct blowing through it,
a household-molded wilderness
that broke free once in a while,
went off into the woods unappeased,
could not be called back.

A Poem about a Refrigerator

(for Cat Doty)

A poem is a windy city, has broad shoulders
& insistent industry,
barrels into your brain, sticking
its steam-filled, swarmy head
into the delicate, empty bird cages
propped in the rooms of your imagination.

A poem can be rude, downright ignorant
of what you had been thinking about
and holding onto for too much of the day.
More than a city, a poem pushes its hemispheres
against your thoughts, knocking them out
of the windows of your ears.
Every good poem screams, "Read me
because you're going to die someday!"

I knew a poem that yelled, "Refrigerator!"
and my brain suddenly had room
for a refrigerator.
For me, it was all Goodbye
tax forms! Goodbye *I wonder if that check bounced!*

My brain was so full of refrigerator—
my mind full of that poem's world—
my whole head suddenly hard on the outside
and suddenly cool on the inside.

Upon Hearing that Baseball is Boring
to America's Youth

(for Ed Romond)

And a tombstone sprouts in Wrigley Field —
    Send flowers to Fenway —
Put a black shroud
    over the house that Ruth built.

Let all the Little League fields
    across Kentucky and Los Angeles
shrivel to brown dead grass
    in the palms of summer —
holy cow, let's just turn 'em
    into golf courses.

The Mick is dead
    and Mel Allen's voice can't be heard
no matter how hard you tune a radio —
    the finesse of your fingertips
    rolling the dial to a frequency
    so thin
        your touch has to be as precise
        as Springtime's
            or Death's —

a finesse you learned on the left side of home plate,
    the ball bearing down
into that slice of percentages, that possibility of heaven
    that's your swing range —
and like a certain coincidence

that occurs with practice,
you connect
        and the crack is like a starter gun
        and your legs start pumping
        before your brain thinks "run"
        and then your brain thinks "run"
        and your legs pump harder
        and there is the ball skating
        somewhere in your left eye
        and you stretch your hamstring
        to the white island of truth
        known as first base
        as the umpire sets up his court there
        and the ball pops into Jimmy's glove
        and you are barely safe
        in this impromptu pick-up game
        that saved you from an afternoon
        of nothing more than not being threatened.

Barely safe was what allowed freedom
in such sport — nothing ever guaranteed
and you had to know everything
going on seventy yards away — an outfield fly
was like a prayer and you were the team's
only angel to catch it. You were salvation.
It was about lining up; it was about advancing
the runner and you working to have a shotgun
arm; it was about no new equipment —
your glove like a pal that moves away
for the winter and returns with the cardinals,

blue jays, and blossoms for a reunion
in the spring. Indeed, each pop fly to you
your glove turned into a blossom, the ball
a bee-line from the sky into the sweet nectar
of out. It was about relying on an old pal.

The team was what mattered —
you did what you did for the greater society of 9
and you knew what you knew for yourself.
Boyhood existed within an outfield fence
and lines that marked foul. Our bases were knapsacks
and library books. Home plate was the Sunday paper —
we swung deep through the news above it.
Baseball wasn't boring; it was what saved us
from boredom. It was about how to swing
with two out and nobody on, how to field
with one out and a man on second. It was
fouling off the great pitches and cutting up
the good pitcher's one bad pitch.
It was how we learned the patience of waiting
and the brooding damage of how even
the subtlest rain could wipe a day away.

It was about myth and spitting, equal parts
of a gentleman's game. It was about
waking up and looking outside and knowing
without a phone call that the other guys
were waking up and knowing without a phone call
to be on the field at 10 — first 18 play first.
It was about feeling the sun on your back

as you watched from the outfield a whole world turning
around the bases, you a distant satellite
ready to relay any message that came.
It was about the game ending and everyone
going to somebody's house to watch Johnny Bench
and Pete Rose and Joe Morgan go up
against anybody else. It was about Thurmon Munson
closing his glove one last time
and that's how boys my age knew what Death was,
and we were able to talk with our grandfathers
about something, play catch with them,
tossing the ball across the wide chasm
the 60's created in everything else. It was about imagining
Steve Carlton pitching Lou Gehrig. Sandy Koufax
pitching to Reggie Jackson. It was about playing
in those games ourselves. It was about tying
the imagination to a hard ball
as it sailed out of Three Rivers and landed
in one of them. It was about hope
in the face of school's fingernails
and winter's long breath. It was about
imagining hope. It was above all
about trying to make it home;
you were a jeweler cutting a diamond's edges
with your body — tagging each base
was like gaining the knowledge you needed
to make it home. And when you dragged
your ankle across the plate's edge,
someone opened his arms
and yelled, "Safe! You're safe!"
and, for that one moment, you were.

Aubade

I love how this morning the world spills
around my breakfast plate, the newspaper opened beneath it—
Kosovo's rebuilding next to my toast
as my mug rests atop the list of celebrity birthdays.
Today's morning is large enough for Alfred Hitchcock and Don Ho
to have the same birthday, both residents now
on the continent of my kitchen table. The coffee machine
warbles its symphony of frogs and radiators
as if to sing of the arrival of the coffee itself.
The fried eggs start applauding.
Before I can stand, Victoria and her green eyes
float into the room and dock on the shores
of my table's new democracy, pouring me a cup.
And I want to be as precise with my joy today
as all those poets are with their suffering.
I want to tell you how on August 13th I was happy
even as the world surrounded my breakfast.
Now I see Fidel Castro and Danny Bonaduce also have
this birthday and they will forever be linked in my mind
with Hitchcock and Don Ho, and that's all right,
because this was the day the coffee and the light and
Victoria's sculptured neckline were pieces of my life breaking
open, and how they conspired to make the world
once more bearable again and again and again.

Bradford Gives a Lecture on the State of Modern Art to a Large, Distinguished Audience

Sometimes what matters is a good answer:
My friend Bradford, thinking Alvin Ailey,
Referred to them as the Alex Haley Dancers.

Some flurries of punches there's no stance for—
They're low and they're high and they're still flailing.
Sometimes a hard swift right is the only answer.

Laughter bloomed over Bradford like cancer—
Each guffaw, a punch, hurt him and ailed me.
He had slipped like an Alex Haley Dancer.

The audience was in a goddamned stir—
How does one count laughter? Does hurt tally?
Desperate in dejection, Bradford answered:

"I got what Hamlet sent Rosencrantz for—
Right here!" During this new soliloquy,
He undid, then yelled, "Hail me—a dancer!"

Some escapes you must get down and prance for;
I know men born in the corners of failing.
When all that mattered was Bradford's answer,
he dropped pants: the newest Alex Haley Dancer.

Upon Being Asked Why I Dedicated My First Book To My Mother When There's Not A Single Poem In There About Her

As Prometheus must have pocketed fire,
slipping it from Olympus in the folds
of his compassion and duplicity,
so my mother stole a Webster's pocket dictionary.
The Mansfield Jamesway Department Store
was all discounts and lighting that refused
to flatter, commerce sliding through its aisles
as my mother slipped that book into her jacket,
getting 30,000 words fatter. I know the arguments—
that's stealing; what about the owner?;
what about teaching her son what's right?
In truth, the entire Jamesway corporation
would go out of business twenty-one years later,
and I'm sure it had to do
with the Webster's Riverside Pocket Dictionary
whose pages held all the words of *Ulysses*
and *Paradise Lost* and *Look Homeward, Angel,*
but jumbled in alphabetical order.
What can I say? She stole a dictionary for me
because there were no words
a judge could use that would be worse
than her son starving
for a lexicon he could grip like a wrench
and loosen all those dumb bolts in his brain.
Receiving that dictionary taught me rectitude
and the many dictates that come down
from its cloistral mountaintop. I was suddenly rich,

a son from the most indigent family in Hampton.
How lucky — when I first started to rub against my language,
sidle up to my own tongue,
my mother stole me a book.
Years later, I gave her one back.

Facetious

What uptight people say
when they want to
say "wise ass."
There it is —*facetious*—
all the vowels aligned
in alphabetical order —
the propriety of protocol.
O to say "Fuck off, wise ass,"
the vowels running backwards
off the wagging precipice
of the tongue, leaping ass-first,
floating every-which-way
on their willy-nilly parachutes.
The horrible, sad decorum
of the man who first came up
with "facetious —" how
he must have been repressing
a smirk as he said it,
tilting his head in the style
of Errol Flynn. A little more tilted,
his smile would run vertical —
a little wise-ass
on the face of facetious.

Pregnant

Like a frigate, she moves through the ice cream aisle,
docks at the frosted doors of the city she has been living in.
She reaches through the Breyers and Good Humor
and plucks out some flavor she's never had
but knows she'll love.   Don't get in her way.
She is doubling in power.   She is potential.
More than a ship, she has become a harbor —
this body of water that will break
onto our sure and otherwise dying earth.

Sex with Emily Dickinson

"I couldn't help myself," I told my wife.
"I was reading her before I went to sleep,
and I can't control what I dream."
"What was it like?" she asked, wearily.
I started quoting *Wild Nights, Wild Nights,*
which she kept saying over and over—Emily, that is—
in the dream, but I didn't mention
the moment of climax
when suddenly Emily turned into Helen Vendler
and told me I was a bad poet.

My wife looked at me
as if my Penis were on trial—
usually the Inquisitor, it was now the Defendant.
"That's okay," she finally smirked, Zero
at the Bone. "There's something I haven't told you.
The first time I read your book,
I dreamt I was in a threesome
with Robert Bly and Robert Penn Warren.
We did it on a huge drum, men in suits
banging in unison around us."
She paused.
"Maybe it was an Iron John thing,"
then "I couldn't help myself."

We sat there awhile, nothing arriving
and nothing leaving, our dreams
causing a caesura of sorts. Finally I said,
"My sex, I'm sure, was more iambic than yours."

"You should know," she rejoined,
"I always hated sex that felt formal."

And we kissed right there, her lips
shaped like the light of a locomotive
at the dark end of a tunnel, which led to touching
which felt like the rumbling of a waiting platform,
which led to great sex, which arrived
like one of those extra trains
they run on holidays.

After it was over we lay there
between the covers — words on opposite pages
finally closed in a book and touching,
which made us a sort of Braille upon each other
there in the dark, reading the language
that rose up from us all night.
A subcutaneous traffic had been loosed
and pulsed along the length of our bed.
As soon as we were Written, we were Read.

Mythology in the Shop-Rite

Not having a boat
or a whimsical chorus of Greek gods,
I am forced to live most of my Homeric epics
at the Shop-Rite in Washington, New Jersey.
And so it was a moment of moral significance
when my Wise Bravos Restaurant-Style Tortilla Chips
scanned at $1.50 instead of the sale price
of 99 cents. Their scanners hooked up to one great body,
like a Cerberus with 3 checkout aisles
guarding purchasing efficiency —
zip zip bag bag beep beep ch-ching
is the background muzak of the subtle hell I entered,
going to "Customer Service," armed with receipt and chips,
and recounted my woes.
                    Evelyn—Price check,
thundered down from the drop ceiling,
and Evelyn appeared.
Five minutes later, having checked,
she said, "No. It's a dollar fifty."
I said, "No!" and asked her to follow.
I was in charge now, armed with receipt and chips
and righteousness and the knowledge a tortuous journey provides.
We arrived at the aisle —I pretended I was Moses,
parting the wall of chips from the wall of soda,
leading Evelyn to the Promised Land, where everything
is priced accurately and Wise chips are only 99 cents.
"Oh, the 10 oz. are 99 cents— you have the 14 oz."
I said, "But then all the 14 oz.'s are behind the 99 cent sign!"
She said, "You should have looked."

"Are you unappeasable!?!" I screamed.
"Is the UPC code the new rock I must push up the hill?
The new eagle plucking at my liver?"
Her mouth parted like clouds:
"All right, I'll give you the 51 cents,
but don't tell anyone."
At the Customer Service counter it was counted —
two quarters and a penny, all of them glinting
like fire I had stolen from the gods
as I crossed the dark parking lot,
four extra ounces of Wise Bravos
than I had ever bargained for.

No Sex

"How long must I kneel before the altar?" I asked.

"Keep crossing yourself," the nun said,
"until you feel forgiven."

4 Metaphors. Nothing More.

There was one moment in my father's life
when he tried to hug me —

It may have been the suddenness of it all —
the usual handshake suddenly with keys in its ignition,
revving up into an embrace —
a collision of our bodies
after the wreckage of my childhood —

He approached — a bear
I had grown comfortable near
with a new, irresistible idea
in its bruin brain —
raising its paws toward me —

and I stood still
but must have shivered slightly away,
as if I were a city
trying to move
its locked-straight buildings
with all their hollow, echoing stairwells
away from an encroaching tidal wave.

The only thing wrong with these metaphors
is that the vehicles missed each other —
or that the bear stopped
because the prey was afraid —
or the tidal wave backed up
        because it somehow knew

the city's infrastructure
with all its strong facades
wrapped around empty spaces
could not sustain such a natural motion.

And there we were in the moment
after that moment in his life —
a man and a man
who happened to be a son and his father —
so close to hugging, standing there quietly,
each second of silence constructing a monument
to the only history we'd ever have —

We were each moths then,
each the other's brilliance —
each of us unsure of soaring
to the source of light we were so close to,
not knowing whether we'd burn
or finally be saved.

For the Children of the World Trade Center Victims

Nothing could have prepared you —

Note: Every poem I have ever written
        is not as important as this one.

Note: This poem says nothing important.

Clarification of last note:
        This poem cannot save 3,000 lives.

Note: This poem is attempting to pull your father
        out of the rubble, still living and glowing
        and enjoying football on Sunday.

Note: This poem is trying to reach your mother
        in her business skirt, and get her home
        to Ridgewood where she can change
        to her robe and sip Chamomile tea
        as she looks through the bay window at the old,
        untouched New York City skyline.

Note: This poem is aiming its guns at the sky
        to shoot down the terrorists and might
        hit God if He let this happen.

Note: This poem is trying to turn
        that blooming of orange and black
        of the impact into nothing
        more than a sudden tiger-lily
        whose petals your mother and father

could use as parachutes, float down
to the streets below, a million
dandelion seeds drifting off
to the untrafficked sky above them.

Note: This poem is still doing nothing.

Note: Somewhere in this poem there may be people alive,
        and I'm trying like mad to reach them.

Note: I need to get back to writing the poem to reach them
        instead of dwelling on these matters, but how
        can any of us get back to writing poems?

Note: The sound of this poem: the sound
        of a scream in 200 different languages
        that outshouts the sounds of sirens and
        airliners and glass shattering and
        concrete crumbling as steel is bending and
        the orchestral tympani of our American hearts
        when the second plane hit.

Note: The sound of a scream in 200 languages
        is the same sound.
        It is the sound of a scream.

Note: In New Jersey over the next four days,
        over thirty people asked me
        if I knew anyone in the catastrophe.

        Yes, I said.
        I knew every single one of them.

No Chaser

The appalling mercy of God —
a daughter is carried for seven and a half months
in the womb — long enough to incubate
the true love of her parents —
and her blood pressure drops.
C-section. The paltry child lives
for thirty seconds and dies
and is placed on her grieving, bleeding
mother's chest. Neither breathed for moments,
then the mother did. As for the kid,
they baptized and buried her.

Did I mention they're friends of mine,
these parents? From childhood, no less.
Why then can I think
only of Richard Hugo, slumping his shoulders
over the mahogany of the Milltown Union Bar?
And now I'm there with him, shooting back
Jack, stunned by the sudden fire on my tonsils,
and he turns and says, "No chaser."
But my throat's aflame and I reach for
the Rheingold but he puts his hand
squarely on my wrist and says,
"Nothing will ever burn you that bad."

Upon Learning That Hearts Can Become Stones

*In South Dakota, a dinosaur heart the size of a grapefruit is said to have
fossilized into reddish/brown stone.* —New York Times (April 21, 2000)

And so scientists have discovered
what bartenders have always known —
given certain conditions and exposure
to harsh elements, even the grandest of hearts
can harden. In the Badlands of South Dakota,
they have discovered not only evident, larger old hearts
but that the smaller stones are hearts too.
We step over the most insignificant ones
all the time, use them to keep shut wind-swept doors,
form perimeters around our gardens.
We imagine how a caveman used a hardened heart
to murder, bring down the blood muscle
of, say, a long-dead horse upon the skull
of someone who done somebody prehistorically wrong.
Scientists today are discovering small chambers
in the middles of cow fields and holding down
liens in law offices, half-hearts broken by prison
chain-gangs, and hearts from way out there
that burned in the night as they approached.
They have been busy identifying, scurrying to discover
the cause of why some hearts burn, others petrify,
but there is no science behind the various geologies
of the heart. So between the dried-up hearts
of fish and the dropping hearts of bats,
we walk toward our own deaths
with our own hearts, our mysteries locked
in these tiny strongboxes that somehow remain.

In the meantime we step on them, we break them,
we spread them on the drives that lead
to our houses. We print them on playing cards
and shuffle them with clubs and spades.
We grind the softest of them to chalk
so that our schoolchildren may learn.

Trash

It was something like love
that called my mother up at 3am
to rise for the *Star-Ledger*—
deliver the papers to the paper deliverers,
her Chevy truck rumbling down Rt. 31,
passing the same cops, the same delivery trucks
heading northbound. It is something like love
that made that memory part of my history—
how many other moments do I have to pull hard on
to remember, like pulling a pike through
swamp water to eat it? Yet that comes so easily,
and now I can say it was love that put potatoes
and spam on the table. And it is love
that makes me cringe at the term "white trash"
because potatoes sometimes were all we could afford
and how we dressed is how we had to dress and I
watched tv a lot because everyone was working
or sleeping off the work and all the money we got
we paid to other white folks who weren't white trash
because they owned used car lots or worked
as loan officers and even though I am the only one
in the family who even went to college or graduate
school or is a professor and author and distinguished
fellow I am still a dopey student of this world
and love my family and how hard they worked and still work
but really worked then just to be called *white trash*
while giving me the wings of encouragement
and "day-old shelf" bread in my soup

to make it and write this poem which I write
because I love them and love them deeply,
old no-good-for-nothin' jagged-toothed white
white white trash that I motherfuckin' am.

Down to a Tune-Up

My father and I peer into the valley of engine —
two survivors on the lips of what might
be a grave — all the hoses and pipes and hard reality
of combustion lying dormant
as we fiddle with what no longer works
well enough to get us somewhere.
We stand upon blocks but also swelling beneath us
as he ponders its power are my childhood
and his inability to even talk outside cracking
a good Irish joke. Like most bar joketellers,
he likes to be liked by a semi-anonymous audience.
But through all those silences and separations,
there was always this: a coming together
to fix an engine: a Fury, a Horizon, two Novas,
all tinkered with and somehow kept alive
for a few thousand more miles, a tire rotation
or two, several million contained explosions
deep in the wells. His father, a mechanic
with the same failure of silence
when a few words would do, more familiar
with the imprecise tools of his hands, not knowing
how precisely a tongue slices through silence.
I am here now, trying to get it all going, knowing
a few jokes myself, a few basics on how to keep
a dying thing running, working with my dad,
smiling with him under the hood, saying the words
that keep us going: *converter, viscosity, timing light,*
snug to a fit, pulling the plug and adjusting the gap.

ACKNOWLEDGMENTS

Acknowledgments and gratitude are due to the editors of these publications in whose pages the following poems (or earlier versions of them) first appeared:

CEREBELLUM: *Aubade; Sex with Emily Dickinson; The Poems I Regret In My First Book; Upon Being Told Again There Are No Rhymes For Certain Words.*

EDISON LITERARY REVIEW: *Pregnant; Upon Being Asked Why I Dedicated My First Book To My Mother When There's Not A Single Poem In There About Her.*

HOME NEWS TRIBUNE: *For the Children of the World Trade Center Victims.*

JOURNAL OF NEW JERSEY POETS: *Education; New Jersey; The Suicidologist.*

KIMERA: *Emperor; Upon Learning That Hearts Can Become Stones; After I Read Sandy Zulauf's "Across the Bar," Victoria Takes Me Skiing.*

LIPS: *Burying Father.*

LONG SHOT: *Down to a Tune-Up; White Trash.*

MAELSTROM: *Facetious; Mythology in the Shop-Rite; No Sex.*

MID-AMERICAN REVIEW: *Another Poem on the Death of a Dog.*

MUSCONETCONG RIVER NEWS: *For Those Who Grew Up on a River.*

NATURAL BRIDGE: *Bradford Gives a Lecture on the State of Modern Art to a Large, Distinguished Audience.*

PAINTED BRIDE QUARTERLY: *Roy Orbison's Last Three Notes.*

PATERSON LITERARY REVIEW: Bandages; Bastards with Badges; Christmas Eve, 1975:What I Realize Now; My Mother's Last Cigarette.

POETRY: The Star-Ledger.

PRAIRIE WINDS: Daily Grind.

PUERTO DEL SOL: Gravedigger's Birthday.

SPITBALL: Upon Hearing that Baseball is Boring to America's Youth.

TRIQUARTERLY: A Poem about a Refrigerator.

U.S. 1 WORKSHEETS: 4 Metaphors, Nothing More; Filling in the New Address Book.

Also, *"Spring Begins in Hinckley, Ohio"* first appeared in *I HAVE MY OWN SONG FOR IT: MODERN POEMS ABOUT OHIO,* published by The University of Akron Press.

"For the Children of the World Trade Center Victims" also appears at *Grounds For Sculpture,* an outdoor sculpture museum in Hamilton, New Jersey, where it has been cast in bronze and acquired as part of the permanent collection.

The following poems also appear in a play, *SHARKS & WHISKY*: *Christmas Eve, 1975:What I Realize Now; The Star-Ledger; Bastards with Badges; My Mother's Last Cigarette; Burying Father; Upon Hearing that Baseball is Boring to America's Youth; 4 Metaphors. Nothing More.; Trash; Bandages;* and *Down To A Tune-Up.*

Thank you to the New Jersey State Council on the Arts for a Distinguished Artist Fellowship that proved essential for the completion of this book. Thanks also to the Virginia Center for the Creative Arts and the Artist/Teacher Institute for the space and time to develop many of these poems. Much gratitude to the Geraldine R. Dodge Foundation and the Alliance for Arts Education/New Jersey for grants that enabled my residencies at the aforementioned artists' colonies.

I'm grateful to the following people whose generosity of spirit has helped in the composition of this book: my family. The beguiling Victoria Reiners. Ben Lapinski (a.k.a. Peter Paul Polanski) for all the hamonica lessons. His son, Ben Lapinski, for the lessons in everything else. Brian Bradford, a Neal Cassady and a Horatio, all in one glorious specimen. Gabrielle Hamilton and Kevin Lopatin for lending — and then giving — me a computer to work on these poems. Grove, Becky, Leo, and everyone at the IKA. Chris and Eric Johnson. Charles Rafferty. Nickole Ingram. Mississippi John Hurt. George Cruys, Byron Williams, and Larry Cantera for teaching this writer about nymphs. Neal Casal, wherever you are. The folks at WNTI. Brian Rumbolo for the cover art and Don Olson for the website. All my teachers — especially Ed, Stephen, Hayden, and Stephen. And, of course, Richard, Lindy, Jan Camp, and everyone at North Atlantic Books — your support has been buoyant.

Typeface notes:

This text has been set in Bembo for the grace of its well-proportioned letterforms and functional serifs. The font was modeled on typefaces cut by Francesco Griffo for Aldus Manutius' printing of De Aetna in 1495 in Venice; the italic is modeled on the hand-writing of the Renaissance scribe Giovanni Tagliente.